# The Countries

# Switzerland

Kristin Van Cleaf

**ABDO Publishing Company**

# visit us at
# www.abdopublishing.com

Published by ABDO Publishing Company, 8000 West 78th Street, Edina, Minnesota 55439.
Copyright © 2008 by Abdo Consulting Group, Inc. International copyrights reserved in all
countries. No part of this book may be reproduced in any form without written permission from the
publisher. The Checkerboard Library™ is a trademark and logo of ABDO Publishing Company.

Printed in the United States.

Interior Photos: Alamy pp. 5, 6, 21, 22, 26, 29, 31, 37; AP Images pp. 25, 27, 33; Corbis pp. 9,
    11, 13, 35; Peter Arnold pp. 18, 19

Editors: Heidi M.D. Elston, Megan M. Gunderson
Art Direction & Maps: Neil Klinepier

## Library of Congress Cataloging-in-Publication Data

Van Cleaf, Kristin, 1976-
  Switzerland / Kristin Van Cleaf.
      p. cm. -- (The countries)
  Includes index.
  ISBN 978-1-59928-786-7
  1. Switzerland--Juvenile literature. I. Title.

DQ17.V36 2008
949.4--dc22
                                    2007010183

# Contents

*Guten Tag, Bonjour, Buon Giorno!* . . . . . . . . . . . . . . . . . 4

Fast Facts. . . . . . . . . . . . . . . . . . . . . . . . . . . 6

Timeline . . . . . . . . . . . . . . . . . . . . . . . . . . . 7

Fighting for Neutrality. . . . . . . . . . . . . . . . . . . 8

Landlocked. . . . . . . . . . . . . . . . . . . . . . . . . 14

Alpine Wildlife . . . . . . . . . . . . . . . . . . . . . . 18

Swiss . . . . . . . . . . . . . . . . . . . . . . . . . . . 20

Banking on Quality . . . . . . . . . . . . . . . . . . . 24

Lively Swiss Cities. . . . . . . . . . . . . . . . . . . . 26

Staying in Touch . . . . . . . . . . . . . . . . . . . . . 28

Swiss Confederation . . . . . . . . . . . . . . . . . . 30

Marking the Seasons . . . . . . . . . . . . . . . . . . 32

Swissness. . . . . . . . . . . . . . . . . . . . . . . . . 34

Glossary . . . . . . . . . . . . . . . . . . . . . . . . . 38

Web Sites . . . . . . . . . . . . . . . . . . . . . . . . 39

Index. . . . . . . . . . . . . . . . . . . . . . . . . . . 40

# *Guten Tag, Bonjour, Buon Giorno!*

Good day from Switzerland! This charming country is tucked among mountains in central Europe. Its people spend much time enjoying adventures in the snowy Swiss Alps. Visitors may even hear some yodeling!

Switzerland is a multicultural country. In fact, it has three official languages. These are German, French, and Italian. Most Swiss speak German. Switzerland also has four national languages. These are the three official languages plus Romansh (roh-MAHNCH). Romansh is related to Old Latin and is spoken in the canton of Graubünden (grow-BOON-duhn).

Switzerland is made up of cantons, which are independent states. The first **alliance** of the cantons began in 1291. The country has only grown since then. Its people value both their independence and their unity. And, they are proud of their country's strong **economy**.

The Swiss flag is a red square with a white cross in the center. For many, it has become a symbol of neutrality and safety. For nearly 200 years, Switzerland has chosen to remain politically neutral, or chosen to not take sides, during international conflicts. As a result, it has long been a refuge for people seeking safety.

**Guten Tag, bonjour, buon giorno**
*from Switzerland!*

# Fast Facts

**OFFICIAL NAME:** Swiss Confederation
**CAPITAL:** Bern

**LAND**
- Area: 15,942 square miles (41,290 sq km)
- Mountain Ranges: Alps, Jura Mountains
- Highest Point: Dufourspitze 15,203 feet (4,634 m)
- Major Rivers: Rhone, Rhine

**PEOPLE**
- Population: 7,554,661 (July 2007 estimate)
- Major Cities: Zürich, Geneva, Basel, Bern
- Languages: German (official), French (official), Italian (official), Romansh
- Religions: Roman Catholicism, Protestantism

**GOVERNMENT**
- Form: Confederation
- Head of State: President
- Head of Government: President
- Legislature: Bicameral Federal Assembly
- Nationhood: August 1, 1291

**ECONOMY**
- Agricultural Products: Grains, fruits, vegetables, meat, eggs
- Manufactured Products: Watches, textiles, chemicals, machinery, precision instruments
- Money: Swiss franc (1 franc = 100 centimes)

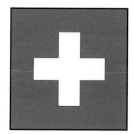

*Switzerland's flag*

*Swiss francs*

# Timeline

| | |
|---|---|
| **850 BC** | Celtic and Raetian tribes are living in Switzerland |
| **58 BC** | The Romans conquer present-day Switzerland |
| **AD 400s** | Germanic tribes put an end to Roman rule in Switzerland |
| **1291** | The Uri, Schwyz, and Unterwalden cantons form an alliance |
| **1798** | France invades Switzerland |
| **1815** | The French are defeated; power is restored to the Swiss cantons; European powers officially recognize Switzerland's neutrality |
| **1848** | Switzerland's constitution is created |
| **1920** | The League of Nations forms in Geneva |
| **1960** | Switzerland helps create the European Free Trade Association |
| **1963** | Switzerland joins the Council of Europe |
| **1971** | All Swiss women receive the right to vote in national elections |
| **1992** | Switzerland joins the International Monetary Fund and the World Bank |
| **2002** | Switzerland becomes a United Nations member |

# Fighting for Neutrality

For thousands of years, people have been calling Switzerland home. Starting around 850 BC, Celtic peoples lived in the west, and Raetian (REE-shee-uhn) peoples lived in the east. Then in 58 BC, Romans conquered the region. They built new cities, enlarged older settlements, and brought in new foods.

By the AD 400s, **Germanic** tribes had moved in, and Roman rule was finished. The Burgundians took over a western area that is now the French-speaking part of Switzerland. The Alemannians pushed Celtic tribes living south of the Rhine River into the Alps. Today, the descendants of these Celts are Switzerland's Romansh speakers.

Present-day Switzerland soon came under control of the **Holy Roman Empire**. The house of Habsburg was one ruling family. Many in the early Swiss cantons feared the Habsburgs gaining too much power.

In July 1291, the first Habsburg ruler of the Holy Roman Empire, Rudolf I, died. Leaders from the cantons of Uri, Schwyz, and Unterwalden saw this as an opportunity. In August, they formed an **alliance**. This was the beginning of the Swiss **Confederation**, which came to be known as Switzerland.

The Habsburgs tried to regain control of Schwyz and Unterwalden in 1315. But, Swiss foot soldiers defeated their army at the Battle of Morgarten. The confederation continued to grow. By 1353, five new cantons had joined the alliance.

*The Romans left their mark throughout Switzerland. An ancient Roman amphitheater still stands at Martigny.*

The Swiss **Confederation** gained many territories through war in the 1400s. And, the **alliance**'s popularity increased. By 1513, there were 13 cantons. The confederation had no central government. So, the cantons governed themselves.

The next years were a time of unrest. Conflicts between **Protestants** and Catholics occurred. Despite this, the cantons were strengthened by the 1648 Peace of Westphalia (vehst-FAYL-yuh). With this, the European powers officially recognized Switzerland's independence.

Switzerland flourished throughout the 1700s. **Textile** industries in wool, cotton, silk, and linen goods increased in importance in several cantons. Embroidery began as an art form. And, clock makers in Geneva gained a good reputation.

In 1798, French armies invaded Switzerland. The French formed the Helvetic Republic to rule the Swiss cantons. But, many Swiss did not want to be ruled by the French. They feared losing rights to a strong central government.

Following French defeat in 1815, power was restored to the individual cantons. And, a small central government was put in place. European powers also recognized Switzerland's neutrality, which has remained ever since.

By 1830, the Swiss had demanded political reform and national unity. In some cantons, governments were overthrown. Many changes occurred peacefully, but a short **civil war** broke out in 1847. In 1848, a new **constitution** created a balance between the central government and the cantons.

*Led by Emperor Napoléon I, France invaded Switzerland on March 5, 1798.*

The new **constitution** resolved many problems among the cantons. The people created uniform money, customs, and weights and measures. And to maintain neutrality and independence, they strengthened their defense system.

When **World War I** broke out, the Swiss declared their neutrality. The fighting countries respected this position. Following the war, Geneva became home to the **League of Nations** in 1920.

Switzerland again declared itself neutral during **World War II**. This neutrality allowed the country to be a refuge for people fleeing war. However, it was surrounded by fighting countries. So at times, the Swiss needed to create **economic** and transportation agreements with the countries at war.

Following the war, the Swiss government participated in international politics that did not threaten its neutrality. In 1960, the Swiss helped create the **European Free Trade Association**. They also joined the **Council of Europe** in 1963.

In 1971, women received the right to vote in national elections. Then in 1981, the Swiss passed an equal rights amendment for women.

*On February 7, 1971, Swiss women were granted the right to vote in national elections.*

Swiss citizens voted to join the **International Monetary Fund** and the **World Bank** in 1992. The **European Union** formed the next year. But Switzerland decided to stay neutral, so it did not join. However, Switzerland became a member of the **United Nations (UN)** in 2002. Today, it remains a neutral but strong member of the world community.

# Landlocked

Switzerland owes its beauty to its harsh yet varied physical features. This mountainous country is about twice the size of New Jersey. Germany is Switzerland's northern neighbor. France borders it to the northwest and west. Italy lies south, and Austria and Liechtenstein (LIHKT-uhn-shtine) are east.

Several large rivers begin in Switzerland. There, the Rhone River begins its journey to the Mediterranean Sea. And, the Rhine River flows north to end in the North Sea.

Switzerland has three main land regions. These are the Jura Mountains, the Swiss **Plateau**, and the Swiss Alps. The most northern region is the Jura Mountains. These rolling mountains run along Switzerland's border with France. Deep valleys separate the limestone ridges.

The Swiss Plateau lies between the Jura Mountains and the Swiss Alps. Its hilly plains hold many lakes. The two largest are Lake Geneva in the southwest and Lake Constance in the northeast. Many of the country's large cities are on the plateau and have a lovely view of the Alps.

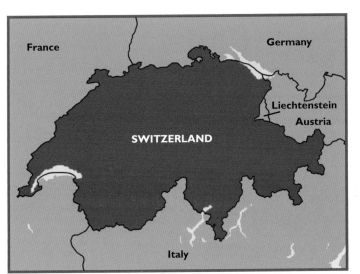

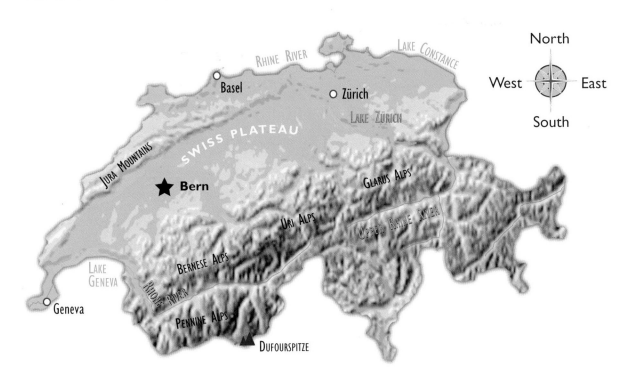

The Swiss Alps cover about 60 percent of Switzerland. They form two side-by-side mountain ranges. The Bernese Alps and the Alps of Uri and Glarus are the northern chain. The Rhone and Rhine river valleys separate them from the southern chain, which includes the Pennine Alps.

In both ranges, the passes are steep and narrow. They can be difficult to travel, depending on the weather and the time of year. The Pennine Alps hold the country's highest point, Dufourspitze (doo-FUR-shpiht-suh). It reaches 15,203 feet (4,634 m) into the sky.

Temperatures and weather vary greatly from the valleys to the mountain peaks. Summer is usually mild. Major cities reach about 77 degrees Fahrenheit (25°C). Rain is common throughout the year.

Winter is usually cold. Average temperatures range from 27 to 32 degrees Fahrenheit (-3 to 0°C). The valleys are often chilly and foggy. But, the mountain slopes get plenty of sun. Snow falls much of the year in the mountains. In those areas, travel is especially dangerous in winter. The alpine region sees about 10,000 **avalanches** in a year.

# Rainfall

## AVERAGE YEARLY RAINFALL

| Inches | | Centimeters |
|--------|---|-------------|
| *Under 20* |  | *Under 50* |
| *20–40* | | *50–100* |
| *40–60* | | *100–150* |
| *Over 60* | | *Over 150* |

# Temperature

## AVERAGE TEMPERATURE

| Fahrenheit | | Celsius |
|------------|---|---------|
| *Over 76°* |  | *Over 24°* |
| *65°–76°* |  | *18°–24°* |
| *54°–65°* |  | *12°–18°* |
| *32°–54°* |  | *0°–12°* |
| *21°–32°* |  | *-6°–0°* |
| *Below 21°* |  | *Below -6°* |

**Rain**

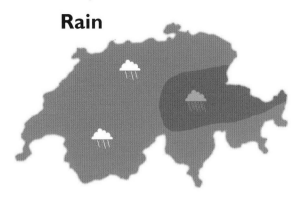

**Winter**

**Summer**

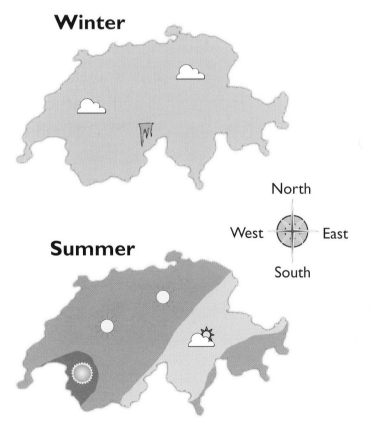

# Alpine Wildlife

Like its climate, Switzerland's plant and animal life vary from one region to another. Large forests of spruce trees cover the northern mountain slopes. Beeches and oaks grow in the west. Groves of chestnut trees are found in the south. And in the east, larch and hornbeam trees are most common.

Mosses and alpine flowers such as edelweiss (AY-duhl-vise) grow above the **timberline**. On the southern mountains, plants are found at higher elevations than on the northern

*Edelweiss*

ranges. This is because there is more sun exposure in the south.

Switzerland's animal life is protected. Hairy, horned goats called ibex died out in the Swiss Alps a number of years ago. But since then, they have been reintroduced.

Large herds of ibex can now be found on Switzerland's mountain slopes.

Chamois (SHA-mee) and marmots live in the mountain meadows. Badgers, foxes, squirrels, rabbits, and deers make their homes in the forests.

Birds such as eagles are also found throughout the country. Snakes and lizards commonly live in the southern lands. And, Switzerland's waters are home to lake and river trout.

*Marmot*

# Swiss

The Swiss have a high standard of living. Family and privacy are important to them. Families are usually small, with couples having only one or two children.

Housing in Switzerland is designed to harmonize with the **environment**. Chalet-style houses are common in rural areas. In the cities, most Swiss families live in apartments or three-bedroom flats.

People in Switzerland eat light breakfasts of cheese, fresh bread, and coffee. For lunch, they generally eat a meat dish with potatoes and a salad. Open-faced sandwiches are common for dinner. For dessert, the Swiss enjoy cakes or fruit pies.

The Swiss are also fond of rich dishes made with potatoes, meat, cheese, or cream. A common potato dish is *rösti*, which is fried, grated potatoes. *Gratin* is sliced potatoes baked with white sauce and cream. Potatoes are also enjoyed french fried and boiled.

The chalet has become a symbol of Switzerland.

Tasty regional specialty foods include sausages, cheeses, leek soup, pork, and fish. And, each canton has its own specialty bread. Many Swiss also enjoy bratwurst, or *saucisse* in French. Popular cheese dishes include fondue and raclette. Raclette is melted cheese served on potato or bread.

The Swiss have freedom of religion. About half the people are Roman Catholic. Most others are **Protestant**. And, about 11 percent of Swiss do not follow any religion.

The Swiss also have an excellent education system. The people enjoy a **99** percent **literacy** rate. Children are required to attend school until they are 15. Then, they may go to gymnasium, or high school. But, students also have the option of attending vocational school to learn a skill or a trade.

Switzerland has several public universities. They are free to all students. The University of Basel, founded in 1469, is the oldest.

*During the cold winter months, Swiss love to gather in restaurants to enjoy fondue.*

# Cheese Rösti

This tasty dish is especially popular served with bratwurst.

- 2 pounds potatoes, boiled in their skins
- 1 1/2 tablespoons butter
- 1/2 cup diced bacon and/or sliced onion
- 2 ounces sliced Gruyère cheese (5–6 slices)

Peel and shred potatoes. Heat butter in skillet. Add potatoes, bacon, and onion as desired, and sprinkle with salt. When a crust begins to form on the bottom, turn over the *rösti*. Top with cheese slices and press down. Cover tightly so the cheese will melt nicely. Cook until golden brown.

AN IMPORTANT NOTE TO THE CHEF: Always have an adult help with the preparation and cooking of food. Never use kitchen utensils or appliances without adult permission and supervision.

LANGUAGE

| English | German | French | Italian |
| --- | --- | --- | --- |
| Good day | Guten Tag (GOO-tehn tahg) | Bonjour (bohn-zhoor) | Buon giorno (bwohn JOHR-noh) |
| Please | Bitte (BIHT-teh) | S'il vous plaît (see voo play) | Per favore (pehr fah-VOH-ray) |
| Thank you | Danke (DAHNG-keh) | Merci (mehr-see) | Grazie (GRAHT-seeay) |
| Yes | Ja (yah) | Oui (wee) | Si (see) |
| Good-bye | Auf Wiedersehen (owf VEE-dehr-zayn) | Au revoir (oh vwahr) | Arrivederci (ah-ree-vay-DEHR-chee) |

# Banking on Quality

Switzerland has one of the world's strongest **economies**. The country has little **unemployment** and poverty. And, the Swiss franc is one of the world's most secure currencies.

Switzerland is famous for its bank system. The nation benefits from its central location, neutrality, and strict privacy laws. These advantages make Switzerland one of the most important financial centers in the world.

Few natural resources are available in Switzerland. So, the Swiss government imports many raw materials. Workers then use these materials to manufacture the country's high-quality exports.

Swiss exports include watches, precision instruments, **textiles**, machinery, and medications. Leather goods, glass, furniture, and **ceramics** are other commonly made items. Germany is one of Switzerland's main trade partners.

Tourism is an important part of the Swiss economy. Visitors provide business for hotels, restaurants, and transportation services.

Only about 10 percent of Switzerland's land is used for raising crops. Farmers grow potatoes, grains, and fruits. Dairy farming is the most important part of Swiss agriculture. Dairy products such as butter and cheese are important exports. The Swiss are also known for their delicious chocolates.

*In the United States, cheese that is sold as "swiss cheese" is not actually from Switzerland. For real Swiss cheese, look for "Emmentaler cheese from Switzerland" on the label.*

# Lively Swiss Cities

Zürich (TSOO-rihk) is Switzerland's largest city. It is ranked as one of the world's most desirable cities to live in.

*Grossmünster in Zürich*

This energetic city lies at the foot of the Alps on the shores of Lake Zürich. Zürich has many beautifully designed buildings and structures. Its **medieval** churches, the Grossmünster and the Fraumünster, should not be missed.

Geneva, the second-largest city, is located near France in southwestern Switzerland. Many international treaties have been worked out in Geneva. And, the **UN** set up its European headquarters there. This paved the way for many international organizations to do the same.

Switzerland's third-largest city is Basel. It is a major port in the north. The Rhine River splits the city into Kleinbasel and Grossbasel. The city's industrial section and the Rhine port are found to the north in Kleinbasel. Grossbasel is the older, **cultural** section located to the south.

Bern is Switzerland's capital and fourth-largest city. This quaint city is a favorite among shoppers and people-watchers. Bern's clock tower is one of its most famous landmarks. Mechanical figurines emerge from the

*Bern's bear pits*

tower and perform four minutes before the hour. The city's bear pits, which provide a home to live bears, are another popular attraction.

# Staying in Touch

Switzerland has a well-developed public transportation system. Buses and trains are common. Fast, modern trains travel through many mountain tunnels. Simplon Tunnel is one of the world's longest railroad tunnels. It is just over 12 miles (19 km) long.

Many Swiss own cars. The land is rough, but the country has a good network of roads. The Saint Gotthard Road Tunnel provides a nearly 11-mile (18-km) route through the Alps. It is one of the longest highway tunnels in the world.

Rivers such as the Rhine provide ship travel. Switzerland has a group of **merchant marine** ships. Steamers are also popular on the country's many lakes. There are few options for flying within Switzerland. But, international airports in Zürich and Geneva welcome visitors from around the world.

The Swiss have many ways to communicate. They can easily telephone or mail letters. Also, most Swiss families own a television and a radio. Programs are broadcast in German, French, and Italian. And, more than 5 million Swiss use the Internet.

There are also about 80 daily newspapers. Most of these are written in German. Others are published in Italian and French. Some nondaily newspapers are available in Romansh.

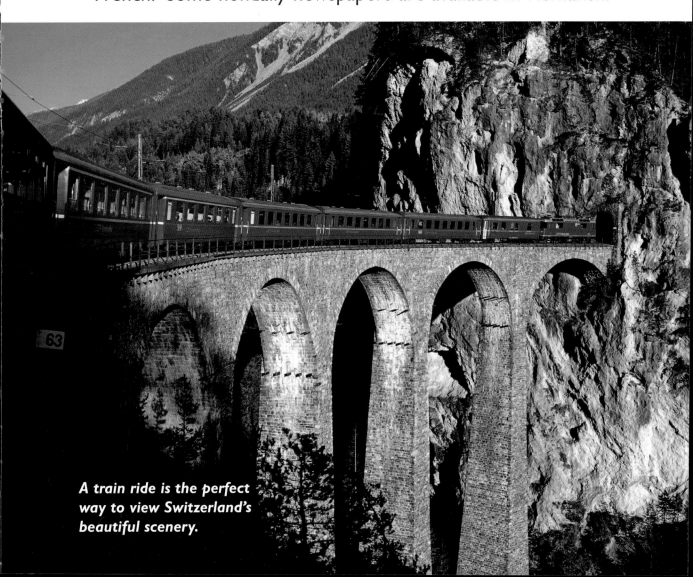

*A train ride is the perfect way to view Switzerland's beautiful scenery.*

# Swiss Confederation

The Swiss **Confederation** adopted its **constitution** in 1848. The government later reworked it in 1874 and 1999. The constitution divides political power between the cantons and the central government.

Each of the 26 cantons controls its education and health care systems. And, each has its own police force. Citizens 18 years or older are able to vote.

The cantons are further divided into about 3,000 communes. The communes vary in size and population. They have their own elected authorities. To gain national citizenship, a person must first be a citizen of a commune.

The central government deals with foreign matters and issues that affect all of the cantons. The executive branch is the Federal Council. The legislature elects seven people to serve on the council for four-year terms. And once a year, the legislature elects council members as the new president and vice president.

The legislative branch is the two-house Federal Assembly. The National Council's 200 members represent the people. The Council of States has 46 members who represent the cantons. Each representative serves a four-year term.

The judicial branch is made up of many small cantonal courts and the country's highest court, the Federal Supreme Court. The Federal Supreme Court hears lower court cases, treason cases, and cases dealing with issues between cantons.

*The Bundeshaus, in Bern, houses the Swiss government.*

# Marking the Seasons

Swiss **culture** is rich with occasions for remembrance and celebration. In the weeks before Easter, the Swiss celebrate carnival. They dress in colorful masks and costumes and parade through the streets playing musical instruments.

Easter is observed from Good Friday through Easter Monday. Chocolate candies and Easter egg hunts have become fun traditions for children. Many villages also decorate with flowers, ribbons, or eggs.

August 1 is Switzerland's National Day. The Swiss remember the day in 1291 that the first cantons joined together. Politicians give speeches and attend meetings on this day. The people celebrate with barbecues, bonfires, and fireworks.

In the mountains, summer's end is marked by farmers bringing their cows home from pasture. This is also a time for harvest. The people hold many festivals, including those for the first wine crops.

*Animal herds come down from the mountains at summer's end. The animals usually have flowers decorating their horns.*

Four Sundays before Christmas Eve, Advent kicks off the Christmas season. During this time, opening Advent calendars and lighting candles on wreaths are Swiss traditions.

On December 6, children check to see if Saint Nicholas filled their shoes with oranges, cookies, and nuts. On Christmas Eve, they see their decorated trees and presents for the first time. Christmas Day is spent relaxing. Then, the Swiss bring in the new year with parties and fireworks.

# Swissness

Switzerland's beautiful mountains offer plenty of activities for the outdoor lover. Almost half of the country's people ski regularly. Many also like to hike, mountain climb, camp, and bobsled. Walking, bicycling, boating, and playing soccer are favorite outdoor activities as well.

A traditional wrestling style called *schwinger* is still popular with some Swiss. *Hornussen* is a traditional game in which a batter uses a club to hit a disk. Then, others try to catch the disk with wooden rackets. Target shooting is a common pastime, too. People in Switzerland also enjoy going to movies and attending **cultural** events and festivals.

Sports and the outdoors are central to Swiss life. But, traditional folk arts are also a strong part of their culture. For example, embroidery is still sewn in many home businesses. The patterns usually decorate shirt cuffs, hats, and scarves.

*Climbing can be done on more than just a rock face. Frozen waterfalls are popular among ice climbers!*

Folk designs also appear in wood carvings. Craftsmen often decorate common objects, such as milking stools, wooden spoons, walking sticks, and bell neck bands. And some artists carve figurines, while others decorate the outsides of houses.

Switzerland's most famous folk art is likely its music. Yodeling is best known. A yodeler sings by quickly raising or lowering his or her voice pitch. Alpenhorns are also associated with Swiss **culture**. These wooden horns can be up to 12 feet (4 m) long! They were originally used to call cows to pasture.

Zürich has a place in art history. The **Dada** art movement began there in 1916. Arts are cherished throughout Switzerland as well. Paul Klee (KLAY) became one of the most talented Swiss painters of the early 1900s.

Sculptor Alberto Giacometti (jahk-aw-MAYT-tee) became famous for his stretched-out figures. And, Jean Tinguely created scrap-metal sculptures that destroyed themselves from their movements.

Some Swiss artists connect themselves with their specific language group. Much Swiss literature has been written in German. Popular works include *Swiss Family Robinson* by Johann Wyss (VEES) and *Heidi* by Johanna Spyri (SHPEE-ree).

Play writers Friedrich Dürrenmatt and Max Frisch are highly celebrated in Switzerland. And, Swiss poet Carl Spitteler won a **Nobel Prize** for Literature. Many devoted Swiss continue to make their country a successful nation.

Today, alpenhorns are used for ceremonies and other traditional events.

# Glossary

**alliance** - people, groups, or nations joined for a common cause.

**avalanche** - a large mass of snow and ice, or dirt and rocks, rapidly sliding or falling down a mountainside.

**ceramic** - of or relating to a nonmetallic product, such as pottery or porcelain.

**civil war** - a war between groups in the same country.

**confederation** - a group united for support or common action.

**constitution** - the laws that govern a country.

**Council of Europe** - a European organization that promotes unity among its members in order to achieve economic and social progress.

**culture** - the customs, arts, and tools of a nation or people at a certain time.

**Dada** - a modern arts movement begun in Switzerland in the early 1900s. It is characterized by the rejection of society's standards and values.

**economy** - the way a nation uses its money, goods, and natural resources.

**environment** - all the surroundings that affect the growth and well-being of a living thing.

**European Free Trade Association** - a trade organization that works to uphold fair trade practices in Western Europe and to remove trade obstacles, such as import and export taxes.

**European Union** - an organization of European countries that works toward political, economic, governmental, and social unity.

**Germanic** - of people of northwestern Europe in the Middle Ages.

**Holy Roman Empire** - a German-based empire in western and central Europe that lasted from AD 962 to 1806.

**International Monetary Fund** - a special agency that works to maintain orderly payment arrangements between countries and to promote worldwide economic growth without inflation.

**League of Nations** - an international association created to maintain peace among the nations of the world.

**literacy** - the state of being able to read and write.
**medieval** - of or belonging to the Middle Ages, which is a period of time from AD 500 to 1500.
**merchant marine** - the ships a country uses in business and the people who operate those ships.
**Nobel Prize** - an award for someone who has made outstanding achievements in his or her field of study.
**plateau** - a raised area of flat land.
**Protestant** - a Christian who does not belong to the Catholic Church.
**textile** - a woven fabric or cloth.
**timberline** - the line beyond which trees will not grow because of the cold.
**unemployment** - the number of people in a country who do not have jobs.
**United Nations (UN)** - a group of nations formed in 1945.  Its goals are peace, human rights, security, and social and economic development.
**World Bank** - an international organization that provides loans to private firms and governments for development projects, such as education and housing.
**World War I** - from 1914 to 1918, fought in Europe.  Great Britain, France, Russia, the United States, and their allies were on one side.  Germany, Austria-Hungary, and their allies were on the other side.
**World War II** - from 1939 to 1945, fought in Europe, Asia, and Africa.  Great Britain, France, the United States, the Soviet Union, and their allies were on one side.  Germany, Italy, Japan, and their allies were on the other side.

# Web Sites

To learn more about Switzerland, visit ABDO Publishing Company on the World Wide Web at **www.abdopublishing.com**. Web sites about Switzerland are featured on our Book Links page. These links are routinely monitored and updated to provide the most current information available.

# Index

**A**
animals  18, 19, 27, 32, 36
architecture  26, 27
arts  10, 34, 35, 36
Austria  14
**C**
cantons  4, 8, 9, 10, 11,
    12, 22, 30, 31, 32
cities  8, 10, 12, 14, 16,
    20, 26, 27, 28, 36
climate  16, 18
communes  30
communication  28, 29
Constance, Lake  14
Council of Europe  12
**E**
economy  4, 10, 12, 20,
    24, 25
education  22, 30
European Free Trade
    Association  12
European Union  13
**F**
festivals  32, 34
food  8, 20, 22, 25, 32, 33
France  10, 14, 26

**G**
Geneva, Lake  14
Germany  8, 14, 24
government  8, 9, 10, 11,
    12, 24, 30, 31
**H**
Habsburgs  8, 9
holidays  32, 33
housing  20, 35
**I**
International Monetary
    Fund  13
Italy  14
**L**
land  4, 8, 14, 16, 18, 19,
    25, 26, 28, 32, 34
language  4, 8, 22, 28, 29,
    36
League of Nations  12
Liechtenstein  14
literature  36
**M**
Mediterranean Sea  14
music  4, 32, 36
**N**
natural resources  24
North Sea  14

**P**
Peace of Westphalia  10
plants  18, 19
**R**
regions  4, 8, 14, 16, 18,
    26, 28
religion  10, 22, 32, 33
Rhine River  8, 14, 16, 27,
    28
Rhone River  14, 16
Rudolf I  8
**S**
sports  34
**T**
transportation  12, 24,
    28
**U**
United Nations  13, 26
**W**
World Bank  13
World War I  12
World War II  12
**Z**
Zürich, Lake  26